GW01311677

BABY LOG

BOOK

BABY log

Date

S M T W T F S

WAKE UP TIME

LAST TIME FED

SLEPT AT

LENGTH OF SLEEP

FEEDING

Start Time	Type of Food	End Time

DIAPER

Time	Pee	Poo

SLEEP TRACKING

Slept @	Note	Woke up

MEDICATIONS

Time	Description

BABY log

Date

S M T W T F S

WAKE UP TIME

LAST TIME FED

SLEPT AT

LENGTH OF SLEEP

FEEDING

Start Time	Type of Food	End Time

DIAPER

Time	Pee	Poo

SLEEP TRACKING

Slept @	Note	Woke up

MEDICATIONS

Time	Description

BABY log

Date

WAKE UP TIME

LAST TIME FED

SLEPT AT

LENGTH OF SLEEP

FEEDING

Start Time	Type of Food	End Time

DIAPER

Time	Pee	Poo

SLEEP TRACKING

Slept @	Note	Woke up

MEDICATIONS

Time	Description

BABY log

Date

WAKE UP TIME

LAST TIME FED

SLEPT AT

LENGTH OF SLEEP

FEEDING

Start Time	Type of Food	End Time

DIAPER

Time	Pee	Poo

SLEEP TRACKING

Slept @	Note	Woke up

MEDICATIONS

Time	Description

BABY log

Date

WAKE UP TIME

LAST TIME FED

SLEPT AT

LENGTH OF SLEEP

FEEDING

Start Time	Type of Food	End Time

DIAPER

Time	Pee	Poo

SLEEP TRACKING

Slept @	Note	Woke up

MEDICATIONS

Time	Description

BABY log

Date

WAKE UP TIME

LAST TIME FED

SLEPT AT

LENGTH OF SLEEP

FEEDING

Start Time	Type of Food	End Time

DIAPER

Time	Pee	Poo

SLEEP TRACKING

Slept @	Note	Woke up

MEDICATIONS

Time	Description

BABY log

Date

WAKE UP TIME

LAST TIME FED

SLEPT AT

LENGTH OF SLEEP

FEEDING

Start Time	Type of Food	End Time

DIAPER

Time	Pee	Poo

SLEEP TRACKING

Slept @	Note	Woke up

MEDICATIONS

Time	Description

BABY log

Date

S M T W T F S

WAKE UP TIME

LAST TIME FED

SLEPT AT

LENGTH OF SLEEP

FEEDING

Start Time	Type of Food	End Time

DIAPER

Time	Pee	Poo

SLEEP TRACKING

Slept @	Note	Woke up

MEDICATIONS

Time	Description

BABY log

Date

S M T W T F S

WAKE UP TIME

LAST TIME FED

SLEPT AT

LENGTH OF SLEEP

FEEDING

Start Time	Type of Food	End Time

DIAPER

Time	Pee	Poo

SLEEP TRACKING

Slept @	Note	Woke up

MEDICATIONS

Time	Description

BABY log

Date

WAKE UP TIME

LAST TIME FED

SLEPT AT

LENGTH OF SLEEP

FEEDING

Start Time	Type of Food	End Time

DIAPER

Time	Pee	Poo

SLEEP TRACKING

Slept @	Note	Woke up

MEDICATIONS

Time	Description

BABY log

Date

S M T W T F S

WAKE UP TIME

LAST TIME FED

SLEPT AT

LENGTH OF SLEEP

FEEDING

Start Time	Type of Food	End Time

DIAPER

Time	Pee	Poo

SLEEP TRACKING

Slept @	Note	Woke up

MEDICATIONS

Time	Description

BABY log

Date

S M T W T F S

WAKE UP TIME

LAST TIME FED

SLEPT AT

LENGTH OF SLEEP

FEEDING

Start Time	Type of Food	End Time

DIAPER

Time	Pee	Poo

SLEEP TRACKING

Slept @	Note	Woke up

MEDICATIONS

Time	Description

BABY log

Date

WAKE UP TIME

LAST TIME FED

SLEPT AT

LENGTH OF SLEEP

FEEDING

Start Time	Type of Food	End Time

DIAPER

Time	Pee	Poo

SLEEP TRACKING

Slept @	Note	Woke up

MEDICATIONS

Time	Description

BABY log

Date

S M T W T F S

WAKE UP TIME

LAST TIME FED

SLEPT AT

LENGTH OF SLEEP

FEEDING

Start Time	Type of Food	End Time

DIAPER

Time	Pee	Poo

SLEEP TRACKING

Slept @	Note	Woke up

MEDICATIONS

Time	Description

BABY log

S M T W T F S

WAKE UP TIME

LAST TIME FED

SLEPT AT

LENGTH OF SLEEP

FEEDING

Start Time	Type of Food	End Time

DIAPER

Time	Pee	Poo

SLEEP TRACKING

Slept @	Note	Woke up

MEDICATIONS

Time	Description

BABY log

Date

WAKE UP TIME

LAST TIME FED

SLEPT AT

LENGTH OF SLEEP

FEEDING

Start Time	Type of Food	End Time

DIAPER

Time	Pee	Poo

SLEEP TRACKING

Slept @	Note	Woke up

MEDICATIONS

Time	Description

BABY log

S M T W T F S

WAKE UP TIME

LAST TIME FED

SLEPT AT

LENGTH OF SLEEP

FEEDING

Start Time	Type of Food	End Time

DIAPER

Time	Pee	Poo

SLEEP TRACKING

Slept @	Note	Woke up

MEDICATIONS

Time	Description

BABY log

Date

S M T W T F S

WAKE UP TIME	
LAST TIME FED	
SLEPT AT	
LENGTH OF SLEEP	

FEEDING

Start Time	Type of Food	End Time

DIAPER

Time	Pee	Poo

SLEEP TRACKING

Slept @	Note	Woke up

MEDICATIONS

Time	Description

BABY log

Date

S M T W T F S

WAKE UP TIME

LAST TIME FED

SLEPT AT

LENGTH OF SLEEP

FEEDING

Start Time	Type of Food	End Time

DIAPER

Time	Pee	Poo

SLEEP TRACKING

Slept @	Note	Woke up

MEDICATIONS

Time	Description

BABY log

Date

S M T W T F S

WAKE UP TIME ....

LAST TIME FED ....

SLEPT AT ....

LENGTH OF SLEEP ....

FEEDING

Start Time	Type of Food	End Time

DIAPER

Time	Pee	Poo
	◯	◯
	◯	◯
	◯	◯
	◯	◯
	◯	◯
	◯	◯
	◯	◯

SLEEP TRACKING

Slept @	Note	Woke up

MEDICATIONS

Time	Description

BABY log

Date

S M T W T F S

WAKE UP TIME

LAST TIME FED

SLEPT AT

LENGTH OF SLEEP

FEEDING

Start Time	Type of Food	End Time

DIAPER

Time	Pee	Poo

SLEEP TRACKING

Slept @	Note	Woke up

MEDICATIONS

Time	Description

BABY log

Date

WAKE UP TIME

LAST TIME FED

SLEPT AT

LENGTH OF SLEEP

FEEDING

Start Time	Type of Food	End Time

DIAPER

Time	Pee	Poo

SLEEP TRACKING

Slept @	Note	Woke up

MEDICATIONS

Time	Description

BABY log

Date

WAKE UP TIME

LAST TIME FED

SLEPT AT

LENGTH OF SLEEP

FEEDING

Start Time	Type of Food	End Time

DIAPER

Time	Pee	Poo

SLEEP TRACKING

Slept @	Note	Woke up

MEDICATIONS

Time	Description

BABY log

Date

WAKE UP TIME

LAST TIME FED

SLEPT AT

LENGTH OF SLEEP

FEEDING

Start Time	Type of Food	End Time

DIAPER

Time	Pee	Poo

SLEEP TRACKING

Slept @	Note	Woke up

MEDICATIONS

Time	Description

BABY log

S M T W T F S

WAKE UP TIME

LAST TIME FED

SLEPT AT

LENGTH OF SLEEP

FEEDING

Start Time	Type of Food	End Time

DIAPER

Time	Pee	Poo

SLEEP TRACKING

Slept @	Note	Woke up

MEDICATIONS

Time	Description

BABY log

Date

WAKE UP TIME

LAST TIME FED

SLEPT AT

LENGTH OF SLEEP

FEEDING

Start Time	Type of Food	End Time

DIAPER

Time	Pee	Poo

SLEEP TRACKING

Slept @	Note	Woke up

MEDICATIONS

Time	Description

BABY log

Date

WAKE UP TIME

LAST TIME FED

SLEPT AT

LENGTH OF SLEEP

FEEDING

Start Time	Type of Food	End Time

DIAPER

Time	Pee	Poo

SLEEP TRACKING

Slept @	Note	Woke up

MEDICATIONS

Time	Description

BABY log

Date

WAKE UP TIME

LAST TIME FED

SLEPT AT

LENGTH OF SLEEP

FEEDING

Start Time	Type of Food	End Time

DIAPER

Time	Pee	Poo

SLEEP TRACKING

Slept @	Note	Woke up

MEDICATIONS

Time	Description

BABY log

Date

S M T W T F S

WAKE UP TIME

LAST TIME FED

SLEPT AT

LENGTH OF SLEEP

FEEDING

Start Time	Type of Food	End Time

DIAPER

Time	Pee	Poo

SLEEP TRACKING

Slept @	Note	Woke up

MEDICATIONS

Time	Description

BABY log

Date

WAKE UP TIME

LAST TIME FED

SLEPT AT

LENGTH OF SLEEP

FEEDING

Start Time	Type of Food	End Time

DIAPER

Time	Pee	Poo

SLEEP TRACKING

Slept @	Note	Woke up

MEDICATIONS

Time	Description

BABY log

Date

WAKE UP TIME

LAST TIME FED

SLEPT AT

LENGTH OF SLEEP

FEEDING

Start Time	Type of Food	End Time

DIAPER

Time	Pee	Poo

SLEEP TRACKING

Slept @	Note	Woke up

MEDICATIONS

Time	Description

BABY log

Date

S M T W T F S

WAKE UP TIME ....

LAST TIME FED ....

SLEPT AT ....

LENGTH OF SLEEP ....

FEEDING

Start Time	Type of Food	End Time

DIAPER

Time	Pee	Poo
	○	○
	○	○
	○	○
	○	○
	○	○
	○	○
	○	○

SLEEP TRACKING

Slept @	Note	Woke up

MEDICATIONS

Time	Description

BABY log

Date

WAKE UP TIME

LAST TIME FED

SLEPT AT

LENGTH OF SLEEP

FEEDING

Start Time	Type of Food	End Time

DIAPER

Time	Pee	Poo

SLEEP TRACKING

Slept @	Note	Woke up

MEDICATIONS

Time	Description

BABY log

Date

WAKE UP TIME

LAST TIME FED

SLEPT AT

LENGTH OF SLEEP

FEEDING

Start Time	Type of Food	End Time

DIAPER

Time	Pee	Poo

SLEEP TRACKING

Slept @	Note	Woke up

MEDICATIONS

Time	Description

BABY log

Date

S M T W T F S

WAKE UP TIME

LAST TIME FED

SLEPT AT

LENGTH OF SLEEP

FEEDING

Start Time	Type of Food	End Time

DIAPER

Time	Pee	Poo

SLEEP TRACKING

Slept @	Note	Woke up

MEDICATIONS

Time	Description

BABY log

Date

S M T W T F S
☐ ☐ ☐ ☐ ☐ ☐ ☐

WAKE UP TIME

LAST TIME FED

SLEPT AT

LENGTH OF SLEEP

FEEDING

Start Time	Type of Food	End Time

DIAPER

Time	Pee	Poo
	◯	◯
	◯	◯
	◯	◯
	◯	◯
	◯	◯
	◯	◯
	◯	◯

SLEEP TRACKING

Slept @	Note	Woke up

MEDICATIONS

Time	Description

BABY log

Date

S M T W T F S

WAKE UP TIME

LAST TIME FED

SLEPT AT

LENGTH OF SLEEP

FEEDING

Start Time	Type of Food	End Time

DIAPER

Time	Pee	Poo

SLEEP TRACKING

Slept @	Note	Woke up

MEDICATIONS

Time	Description

BABY log

Date

S M T W T F S

WAKE UP TIME

LAST TIME FED

SLEPT AT

LENGTH OF SLEEP

FEEDING

Start Time	Type of Food	End Time

DIAPER

Time	Pee	Poo

SLEEP TRACKING

Slept @	Note	Woke up

MEDICATIONS

Time	Description

BABY log

Date

S M T W T F S

WAKE UP TIME

LAST TIME FED

SLEPT AT

LENGTH OF SLEEP

FEEDING

Start Time	Type of Food	End Time

DIAPER

Time	Pee	Poo

SLEEP TRACKING

Slept @	Note	Woke up

MEDICATIONS

Time	Description

BABY log

Date

WAKE UP TIME

LAST TIME FED

SLEPT AT

LENGTH OF SLEEP

FEEDING

Start Time	Type of Food	End Time

DIAPER

Time	Pee	Poo

SLEEP TRACKING

Slept @	Note	Woke up

MEDICATIONS

Time	Description

BABY log

Date

S	M	T	W	T	F	S

WAKE UP TIME

LAST TIME FED

SLEPT AT

LENGTH OF SLEEP

FEEDING

Start Time	Type of Food	End Time

DIAPER

Time	Pee	Poo

SLEEP TRACKING

Slept @	Note	Woke up

MEDICATIONS

Time	Description

BABY log

Date

S M T W T F S

WAKE UP TIME	
LAST TIME FED	
SLEPT AT	
LENGTH OF SLEEP	

FEEDING

Start Time	Type of Food	End Time

DIAPER

Time	Pee	Poo
	○	○
	○	○
	○	○
	○	○
	○	○
	○	○
	○	○

SLEEP TRACKING

Slept @	Note	Woke up

MEDICATIONS

Time	Description

BABY log

Date

WAKE UP TIME

LAST TIME FED

SLEPT AT

LENGTH OF SLEEP

FEEDING

Start Time	Type of Food	End Time

DIAPER

Time	Pee	Poo

SLEEP TRACKING

Slept @	Note	Woke up

MEDICATIONS

Time	Description

BABY log

Date

WAKE UP TIME

LAST TIME FED

SLEPT AT

LENGTH OF SLEEP

FEEDING

Start Time	Type of Food	End Time

DIAPER

Time	Pee	Poo
	◯	◯
	◯	◯
	◯	◯
	◯	◯
	◯	◯
	◯	◯
	◯	◯

SLEEP TRACKING

Slept @	Note	Woke up

MEDICATIONS

Time	Description

BABY log

Date

S M T W T F S

WAKE UP TIME

LAST TIME FED

SLEPT AT

LENGTH OF SLEEP

FEEDING

Start Time	Type of Food	End Time

DIAPER

Time	Pee	Poo

SLEEP TRACKING

Slept @	Note	Woke up

MEDICATIONS

Time	Description

BABY log

Date

WAKE UP TIME

LAST TIME FED

SLEPT AT

LENGTH OF SLEEP

FEEDING

Start Time	Type of Food	End Time

DIAPER

Time	Pee	Poo
	◯	◯
	◯	◯
	◯	◯
	◯	◯
	◯	◯
	◯	◯
	◯	◯

SLEEP TRACKING

Slept @	Note	Woke up

MEDICATIONS

Time	Description

BABY log

Date

S M T W T F S

WAKE UP TIME

LAST TIME FED

SLEPT AT

LENGTH OF SLEEP

FEEDING

Start Time	Type of Food	End Time

DIAPER

Time	Pee	Poo

SLEEP TRACKING

Slept @	Note	Woke up

MEDICATIONS

Time	Description

BABY log

S M T W T F S

WAKE UP TIME

LAST TIME FED

SLEPT AT

LENGTH OF SLEEP

FEEDING

Start Time	Type of Food	End Time

DIAPER

Time	Pee	Poo

SLEEP TRACKING

Slept @	Note	Woke up

MEDICATIONS

Time	Description

BABY log

Date

S M T W T F S

WAKE UP TIME

LAST TIME FED

SLEPT AT

LENGTH OF SLEEP

FEEDING

Start Time	Type of Food	End Time

DIAPER

Time	Pee	Poo

SLEEP TRACKING

Slept @	Note	Woke up

MEDICATIONS

Time	Description

BABY log

Date

S M T W T F S

WAKE UP TIME ....

LAST TIME FED ....

SLEPT AT ....

LENGTH OF SLEEP ....

FEEDING

Start Time	Type of Food	End Time

DIAPER

Time	Pee	Poo

SLEEP TRACKING

Slept @	Note	Woke up

MEDICATIONS

Time	Description

BABY log

Date

S M T W T F S

WAKE UP TIME

LAST TIME FED

SLEPT AT

LENGTH OF SLEEP

FEEDING

Start Time	Type of Food	End Time

DIAPER

Time	Pee	Poo

SLEEP TRACKING

Slept @	Note	Woke up

MEDICATIONS

Time	Description

BABY log

Date

WAKE UP TIME

LAST TIME FED

SLEPT AT

LENGTH OF SLEEP

FEEDING

Start Time	Type of Food	End Time

DIAPER

Time	Pee	Poo

SLEEP TRACKING

Slept @	Note	Woke up

MEDICATIONS

Time	Description

BABY log

Date

WAKE UP TIME

LAST TIME FED

SLEPT AT

LENGTH OF SLEEP

FEEDING

Start Time	Type of Food	End Time

DIAPER

Time	Pee	Poo

SLEEP TRACKING

Slept @	Note	Woke up

MEDICATIONS

Time	Description

BABY log

Date

WAKE UP TIME

LAST TIME FED

SLEPT AT

LENGTH OF SLEEP

FEEDING

Start Time	Type of Food	End Time

DIAPER

Time	Pee	Poo

SLEEP TRACKING

Slept @	Note	Woke up

MEDICATIONS

Time	Description

BABY log

Date

S M T W T F S

WAKE UP TIME

LAST TIME FED

SLEPT AT

LENGTH OF SLEEP

FEEDING

Start Time	Type of Food	End Time

DIAPER

Time	Pee	Poo

SLEEP TRACKING

Slept @	Note	Woke up

MEDICATIONS

Time	Description

BABY log

S M T W T F S

WAKE UP TIME

LAST TIME FED

SLEPT AT

LENGTH OF SLEEP

FEEDING

Start Time	Type of Food	End Time

DIAPER

Time	Pee	Poo

SLEEP TRACKING

Slept @	Note	Woke up

MEDICATIONS

Time	Description

BABY log

Date

WAKE UP TIME

LAST TIME FED

SLEPT AT

LENGTH OF SLEEP

FEEDING

Start Time	Type of Food	End Time

DIAPER

Time	Pee	Poo

SLEEP TRACKING

Slept @	Note	Woke up

MEDICATIONS

Time	Description

BABY log

Date

S M T W T F S

WAKE UP TIME

LAST TIME FED

SLEPT AT

LENGTH OF SLEEP

FEEDING

Start Time	Type of Food	End Time

DIAPER

Time	Pee	Poo

SLEEP TRACKING

Slept @	Note	Woke up

MEDICATIONS

Time	Description

BABY log

S M T W T F S

WAKE UP TIME

LAST TIME FED

SLEPT AT

LENGTH OF SLEEP

FEEDING

Start Time	Type of Food	End Time

DIAPER

Time	Pee	Poo

SLEEP TRACKING

Slept @	Note	Woke up

MEDICATIONS

Time	Description

BABY log

S M T W T F S

WAKE UP TIME

LAST TIME FED

SLEPT AT

LENGTH OF SLEEP

FEEDING

Start Time	Type of Food	End Time

DIAPER

Time	Pee	Poo
	◯	◯
	◯	◯
	◯	◯
	◯	◯
	◯	◯
	◯	◯
	◯	◯

SLEEP TRACKING

Slept @	Note	Woke up

MEDICATIONS

Time	Description

BABY log

Date

S M T W T F S

WAKE UP TIME

LAST TIME FED

SLEPT AT

LENGTH OF SLEEP

FEEDING

Start Time	Type of Food	End Time

DIAPER

Time	Pee	Poo

SLEEP TRACKING

Slept @	Note	Woke up

MEDICATIONS

Time	Description

BABY log

Date

WAKE UP TIME

LAST TIME FED

SLEPT AT

LENGTH OF SLEEP

FEEDING

Start Time	Type of Food	End Time

DIAPER

Time	Pee	Poo

SLEEP TRACKING

Slept @	Note	Woke up

MEDICATIONS

Time	Description

BABY log

Date

WAKE UP TIME

LAST TIME FED

SLEPT AT

LENGTH OF SLEEP

FEEDING

Start Time	Type of Food	End Time

DIAPER

Time	Pee	Poo

SLEEP TRACKING

Slept @	Note	Woke up

MEDICATIONS

Time	Description

BABY log

WAKE UP TIME ....

LAST TIME FED ....

SLEPT AT ....

LENGTH OF SLEEP ....

S M T W T F S

FEEDING

Start Time	Type of Food	End Time

DIAPER

Time	Pee	Poo

SLEEP TRACKING

Slept @	Note	Woke up

MEDICATIONS

Time	Description

BABY log

Date

S M T W T F S

WAKE UP TIME

LAST TIME FED

SLEPT AT

LENGTH OF SLEEP

FEEDING

Start Time	Type of Food	End Time

DIAPER

Time	Pee	Poo

SLEEP TRACKING

Slept @	Note	Woke up

MEDICATIONS

Time	Description

BABY log

Date

WAKE UP TIME

LAST TIME FED

SLEPT AT

LENGTH OF SLEEP

FEEDING

Start Time	Type of Food	End Time

DIAPER

Time	Pee	Poo

SLEEP TRACKING

Slept @	Note	Woke up

MEDICATIONS

Time	Description

BABY log

Date

WAKE UP TIME

LAST TIME FED

SLEPT AT

LENGTH OF SLEEP

FEEDING

Start Time	Type of Food	End Time

DIAPER

Time	Pee	Poo

SLEEP TRACKING

Slept @	Note	Woke up

MEDICATIONS

Time	Description

BABY log

Date

S	M	T	W	T	F	S

WAKE UP TIME

LAST TIME FED

SLEPT AT

LENGTH OF SLEEP

FEEDING

Start Time	Type of Food	End Time

DIAPER

Time	Pee	Poo

SLEEP TRACKING

Slept @	Note	Woke up

MEDICATIONS

Time	Description

BABY log

Date

WAKE UP TIME

LAST TIME FED

SLEPT AT

LENGTH OF SLEEP

FEEDING

Start Time	Type of Food	End Time

DIAPER

Time	Pee	Poo

SLEEP TRACKING

Slept @	Note	Woke up

MEDICATIONS

Time	Description

BABY log

Date

WAKE UP TIME

LAST TIME FED

SLEPT AT

LENGTH OF SLEEP

FEEDING

Start Time	Type of Food	End Time

DIAPER

Time	Pee	Poo

SLEEP TRACKING

Slept @	Note	Woke up

MEDICATIONS

Time	Description

BABY log

Date

WAKE UP TIME

LAST TIME FED

SLEPT AT

LENGTH OF SLEEP

FEEDING

Start Time	Type of Food	End Time

DIAPER

Time	Pee	Poo

SLEEP TRACKING

Slept @	Note	Woke up

MEDICATIONS

Time	Description

BABY log

S M T W T F S

WAKE UP TIME

LAST TIME FED

SLEPT AT

LENGTH OF SLEEP

FEEDING

Start Time	Type of Food	End Time

DIAPER

Time	Pee	Poo

SLEEP TRACKING

Slept @	Note	Woke up

MEDICATIONS

Time	Description

BABY log

Date

WAKE UP TIME

LAST TIME FED

SLEPT AT

LENGTH OF SLEEP

FEEDING

Start Time	Type of Food	End Time

DIAPER

Time	Pee	Poo

SLEEP TRACKING

Slept @	Note	Woke up

MEDICATIONS

Time	Description

BABY log

Date

S M T W T F S

WAKE UP TIME

LAST TIME FED

SLEPT AT

LENGTH OF SLEEP

FEEDING

Start Time	Type of Food	End Time

DIAPER

Time	Pee	Poo

SLEEP TRACKING

Slept @	Note	Woke up

MEDICATIONS

Time	Description

BABY log

Date

S M T W T F S

WAKE UP TIME

LAST TIME FED

SLEPT AT

LENGTH OF SLEEP

FEEDING

Start Time	Type of Food	End Time

DIAPER

Time	Pee	Poo

SLEEP TRACKING

Slept @	Note	Woke up

MEDICATIONS

Time	Description

BABY log

Date

S M T W T F S

WAKE UP TIME

LAST TIME FED

SLEPT AT

LENGTH OF SLEEP

FEEDING

Start Time	Type of Food	End Time

DIAPER

Time	Pee	Poo

SLEEP TRACKING

Slept @	Note	Woke up

MEDICATIONS

Time	Description

BABY log

Date

S M T W T F S

WAKE UP TIME

LAST TIME FED

SLEPT AT

LENGTH OF SLEEP

FEEDING

Start Time	Type of Food	End Time

DIAPER

Time	Pee	Poo

SLEEP TRACKING

Slept @	Note	Woke up

MEDICATIONS

Time	Description

BABY log

Date

WAKE UP TIME

LAST TIME FED

SLEPT AT

LENGTH OF SLEEP

FEEDING

Start Time	Type of Food	End Time

DIAPER

Time	Pee	Poo

SLEEP TRACKING

Slept @	Note	Woke up

MEDICATIONS

Time	Description

BABY log

Date

S M T W T F S

WAKE UP TIME

LAST TIME FED

SLEPT AT

LENGTH OF SLEEP

FEEDING

Start Time	Type of Food	End Time

DIAPER

Time	Pee	Poo

SLEEP TRACKING

Slept @	Note	Woke up

MEDICATIONS

Time	Description

BABY log

Date

S M T W T F S

WAKE UP TIME

LAST TIME FED

SLEPT AT

LENGTH OF SLEEP

FEEDING

Start Time	Type of Food	End Time

DIAPER

Time	Pee	Poo

SLEEP TRACKING

Slept @	Note	Woke up

MEDICATIONS

Time	Description

BABY log

S M T W T F S

WAKE UP TIME

LAST TIME FED

SLEPT AT

LENGTH OF SLEEP

FEEDING

Start Time	Type of Food	End Time

DIAPER

Time	Pee	Poo

SLEEP TRACKING

Slept @	Note	Woke up

MEDICATIONS

Time	Description

BABY log

Date

WAKE UP TIME

LAST TIME FED

SLEPT AT

LENGTH OF SLEEP

FEEDING

Start Time	Type of Food	End Time

DIAPER

Time	Pee	Poo

SLEEP TRACKING

Slept @	Note	Woke up

MEDICATIONS

Time	Description

BABY log

Date

S M T W T F S

WAKE UP TIME

LAST TIME FED

SLEPT AT

LENGTH OF SLEEP

FEEDING

Start Time	Type of Food	End Time

DIAPER

Time	Pee	Poo

SLEEP TRACKING

Slept @	Note	Woke up

MEDICATIONS

Time	Description

BABY log

Date

S M T W T F S

WAKE UP TIME

LAST TIME FED

SLEPT AT

LENGTH OF SLEEP

FEEDING

Start Time	Type of Food	End Time

DIAPER

Time	Pee	Poo

SLEEP TRACKING

Slept @	Note	Woke up

MEDICATIONS

Time	Description

BABY log

Date

WAKE UP TIME

LAST TIME FED

SLEPT AT

LENGTH OF SLEEP

FEEDING

Start Time	Type of Food	End Time

DIAPER

Time	Pee	Poo

SLEEP TRACKING

Slept @	Note	Woke up

MEDICATIONS

Time	Description

BABY log

Date

WAKE UP TIME

LAST TIME FED

SLEPT AT

LENGTH OF SLEEP

FEEDING

Start Time	Type of Food	End Time

DIAPER

Time	Pee	Poo

SLEEP TRACKING

Slept @	Note	Woke up

MEDICATIONS

Time	Description

BABY log

Date

S M T W T F S

WAKE UP TIME

LAST TIME FED

SLEPT AT

LENGTH OF SLEEP

FEEDING

Start Time	Type of Food	End Time

DIAPER

Time	Pee	Poo

SLEEP TRACKING

Slept @	Note	Woke up

MEDICATIONS

Time	Description

BABY log

Date

WAKE UP TIME

LAST TIME FED

SLEPT AT

LENGTH OF SLEEP

FEEDING

Start Time	Type of Food	End Time

DIAPER

Time	Pee	Poo

SLEEP TRACKING

Slept @	Note	Woke up

MEDICATIONS

Time	Description

BABY log

Date

S M T W T F S

WAKE UP TIME

LAST TIME FED

SLEPT AT

LENGTH OF SLEEP

FEEDING

Start Time	Type of Food	End Time

DIAPER

Time	Pee	Poo

SLEEP TRACKING

Slept @	Note	Woke up

MEDICATIONS

Time	Description

BABY log

Date

S M T W T F S

WAKE UP TIME

LAST TIME FED

SLEPT AT

LENGTH OF SLEEP

FEEDING

Start Time	Type of Food	End Time

DIAPER

Time	Pee	Poo

SLEEP TRACKING

Slept @	Note	Woke up

MEDICATIONS

Time	Description

BABY log

Date

WAKE UP TIME

LAST TIME FED

SLEPT AT

LENGTH OF SLEEP

FEEDING

Start Time	Type of Food	End Time

DIAPER

Time	Pee	Poo

SLEEP TRACKING

Slept @	Note	Woke up

MEDICATIONS

Time	Description

BABY log

Date _____

WAKE UP TIME ....

LAST TIME FED ....

SLEPT AT ....

LENGTH OF SLEEP ....

FEEDING

Start Time	Type of Food	End Time

DIAPER

Time	Pee	Poo
	○	○
	○	○
	○	○
	○	○
	○	○
	○	○
	○	○

SLEEP TRACKING

Slept @	Note	Woke up

MEDICATIONS

Time	Description

BABY log

Date

S M T W T F S

WAKE UP TIME

LAST TIME FED

SLEPT AT

LENGTH OF SLEEP

FEEDING

Start Time	Type of Food	End Time

DIAPER

Time	Pee	Poo

SLEEP TRACKING

Slept @	Note	Woke up

MEDICATIONS

Time	Description

BABY log

Date

S M T W T F S

WAKE UP TIME	
LAST TIME FED	
SLEPT AT	
LENGTH OF SLEEP	

FEEDING

Start Time	Type of Food	End Time

DIAPER

Time	Pee	Poo

SLEEP TRACKING

Slept @	Note	Woke up

MEDICATIONS

Time	Description

BABY log

Date

S M T W T F S

WAKE UP TIME

LAST TIME FED

SLEPT AT

LENGTH OF SLEEP

FEEDING

Start Time	Type of Food	End Time

DIAPER

Time	Pee	Poo

SLEEP TRACKING

Slept @	Note	Woke up

MEDICATIONS

Time	Description

BABY log

S M T W T F S

WAKE UP TIME

LAST TIME FED

SLEPT AT

LENGTH OF SLEEP

FEEDING

Start Time	Type of Food	End Time

DIAPER

Time	Pee	Poo

SLEEP TRACKING

Slept @	Note	Woke up

MEDICATIONS

Time	Description

BABY log

Date

WAKE UP TIME

LAST TIME FED

SLEPT AT

LENGTH OF SLEEP

FEEDING

Start Time	Type of Food	End Time

DIAPER

Time	Pee	Poo
	○	○
	○	○
	○	○
	○	○
	○	○
	○	○
	○	○

SLEEP TRACKING

Slept @	Note	Woke up

MEDICATIONS

Time	Description

BABY log

S M T W T F S

WAKE UP TIME

LAST TIME FED

SLEPT AT

LENGTH OF SLEEP

FEEDING

Start Time	Type of Food	End Time

DIAPER

Time	Pee	Poo
	○	○
	○	○
	○	○
	○	○
	○	○
	○	○
	○	○

SLEEP TRACKING

Slept @	Note	Woke up

MEDICATIONS

Time	Description

BABY log

Date

WAKE UP TIME

LAST TIME FED

SLEPT AT

LENGTH OF SLEEP

FEEDING

Start Time	Type of Food	End Time

DIAPER

Time	Pee	Poo

SLEEP TRACKING

Slept @	Note	Woke up

MEDICATIONS

Time	Description

BABY log

S M T W T F S

WAKE UP TIME

LAST TIME FED

SLEPT AT

LENGTH OF SLEEP

FEEDING

Start Time	Type of Food	End Time

DIAPER

Time	Pee	Poo

SLEEP TRACKING

Slept @	Note	Woke up

MEDICATIONS

Time	Description

BABY log

Date

S M T W T F S

WAKE UP TIME

LAST TIME FED

SLEPT AT

LENGTH OF SLEEP

FEEDING

Start Time	Type of Food	End Time

DIAPER

Time	Pee	Poo
	◯	◯
	◯	◯
	◯	◯
	◯	◯
	◯	◯
	◯	◯
	◯	◯

SLEEP TRACKING

Slept @	Note	Woke up

MEDICATIONS

Time	Description

BABY log

S M T W T F S

WAKE UP TIME

LAST TIME FED

SLEPT AT

LENGTH OF SLEEP

FEEDING

Start Time	Type of Food	End Time

DIAPER

Time	Pee	Poo

SLEEP TRACKING

Slept @	Note	Woke up

MEDICATIONS

Time	Description

BABY log

Date

S M T W T F S

WAKE UP TIME

LAST TIME FED

SLEPT AT

LENGTH OF SLEEP

FEEDING

Start Time	Type of Food	End Time

DIAPER

Time	Pee	Poo

SLEEP TRACKING

Slept @	Note	Woke up

MEDICATIONS

Time	Description

BABY log

Date

S M T W T F S

WAKE UP TIME

LAST TIME FED

SLEPT AT

LENGTH OF SLEEP

FEEDING

Start Time	Type of Food	End Time

DIAPER

Time	Pee	Poo

SLEEP TRACKING

Slept @	Note	Woke up

MEDICATIONS

Time	Description

BABY log

Date

S M T W T F S

WAKE UP TIME

LAST TIME FED

SLEPT AT

LENGTH OF SLEEP

FEEDING

Start Time	Type of Food	End Time

DIAPER

Time	Pee	Poo

SLEEP TRACKING

Slept @	Note	Woke up

MEDICATIONS

Time	Description

BABY log

Date

S M T W T F S

WAKE UP TIME

LAST TIME FED

SLEPT AT

LENGTH OF SLEEP

FEEDING

Start Time	Type of Food	End Time

DIAPER

Time	Pee	Poo
	◯	◯
	◯	◯
	◯	◯
	◯	◯
	◯	◯
	◯	◯
	◯	◯

SLEEP TRACKING

Slept @	Note	Woke up

MEDICATIONS

Time	Description

BABY log

Date

WAKE UP TIME

LAST TIME FED

SLEPT AT

LENGTH OF SLEEP

FEEDING

Start Time	Type of Food	End Time

DIAPER

Time	Pee	Poo

SLEEP TRACKING

Slept @	Note	Woke up

MEDICATIONS

Time	Description

BABY log

Date

WAKE UP TIME

LAST TIME FED

SLEPT AT

LENGTH OF SLEEP

FEEDING

Start Time	Type of Food	End Time

DIAPER

Time	Pee	Poo

SLEEP TRACKING

Slept @	Note	Woke up

MEDICATIONS

Time	Description

BABY log

Date

S M T W T F S

WAKE UP TIME

LAST TIME FED

SLEPT AT

LENGTH OF SLEEP

FEEDING

Start Time	Type of Food	End Time

DIAPER

Time	Pee	Poo

SLEEP TRACKING

Slept @	Note	Woke up

MEDICATIONS

Time	Description

BABY log

Date

S M T W T F S

WAKE UP TIME

LAST TIME FED

SLEPT AT

LENGTH OF SLEEP

FEEDING

Start Time	Type of Food	End Time

DIAPER

Time	Pee	Poo

SLEEP TRACKING

Slept @	Note	Woke up

MEDICATIONS

Time	Description

BABY log

Date

S M T W T F S

WAKE UP TIME

LAST TIME FED

SLEPT AT

LENGTH OF SLEEP

FEEDING

Start Time	Type of Food	End Time

DIAPER

Time	Pee	Poo

SLEEP TRACKING

Slept @	Note	Woke up

MEDICATIONS

Time	Description

BABY log

Date

S M T W T F S

WAKE UP TIME

LAST TIME FED

SLEPT AT

LENGTH OF SLEEP

FEEDING

Start Time	Type of Food	End Time

DIAPER

Time	Pee	Poo

SLEEP TRACKING

Slept @	Note	Woke up

MEDICATIONS

Time	Description

BABY log

Date

S M T W T F S

WAKE UP TIME

LAST TIME FED

SLEPT AT

LENGTH OF SLEEP

FEEDING

Start Time	Type of Food	End Time

DIAPER

Time	Pee	Poo

SLEEP TRACKING

Slept @	Note	Woke up

MEDICATIONS

Time	Description

BABY log

Date

S M T W T F S

WAKE UP TIME

LAST TIME FED

SLEPT AT

LENGTH OF SLEEP

FEEDING

Start Time	Type of Food	End Time

DIAPER

Time	Pee	Poo

SLEEP TRACKING

Slept @	Note	Woke up

MEDICATIONS

Time	Description

BABY log

Date

WAKE UP TIME

LAST TIME FED

SLEPT AT

LENGTH OF SLEEP

FEEDING

Start Time	Type of Food	End Time

DIAPER

Time	Pee	Poo

SLEEP TRACKING

Slept @	Note	Woke up

MEDICATIONS

Time	Description

BABY log

Date

S M T W T F S

WAKE UP TIME

LAST TIME FED

SLEPT AT

LENGTH OF SLEEP

FEEDING

Start Time	Type of Food	End Time

DIAPER

Time	Pee	Poo

SLEEP TRACKING

Slept @	Note	Woke up

MEDICATIONS

Time	Description

BABY log

Date

S M T W T F S

WAKE UP TIME

LAST TIME FED

SLEPT AT

LENGTH OF SLEEP

FEEDING

Start Time	Type of Food	End Time

DIAPER

Time	Pee	Poo

SLEEP TRACKING

Slept @	Note	Woke up

MEDICATIONS

Time	Description

BABY log

Date

S M T W T F S

WAKE UP TIME

LAST TIME FED

SLEPT AT

LENGTH OF SLEEP

FEEDING

Start Time	Type of Food	End Time

DIAPER

Time	Pee	Poo

SLEEP TRACKING

Slept @	Note	Woke up

MEDICATIONS

Time	Description

BABY log

Date

WAKE UP TIME

LAST TIME FED

SLEPT AT

LENGTH OF SLEEP

FEEDING

Start Time	Type of Food	End Time

DIAPER

Time	Pee	Poo
	◯	◯
	◯	◯
	◯	◯
	◯	◯
	◯	◯
	◯	◯
	◯	◯

SLEEP TRACKING

Slept @	Note	Woke up

MEDICATIONS

Time	Description

BABY log

S M T W T F S

WAKE UP TIME

LAST TIME FED

SLEPT AT

LENGTH OF SLEEP

FEEDING

Start Time	Type of Food	End Time

DIAPER

Time	Pee	Poo

SLEEP TRACKING

Slept @	Note	Woke up

MEDICATIONS

Time	Description